ESSENTIAL KNOTS & RIGS FOR TROUT

Joe Mahler

HeadWater
Books

STACKPOLE
BOOKS

Published by
STACKPOLE BOOKS
5067 Ritter Road
Mechanicsburg, PA 17055
www.stackpolebooks.com

Printed in the United States of America

First edition

10 9 8 7 6 5 4 3 2

Illustrations by the author
Cover design by Caroline M. Stover

Library of Congress Cataloging-in-Publication Data

Mahler, Joe.
  Essential knots and rigs for trout / Joe Mahler. — 1st ed.
      p. cm.
  Includes index.
  ISBN-13: 978-0-8117-0716-9
  ISBN-10: 0-8117-0716-4
  1. Trout fishing. 2. Fishing rigs. I. Title.
  SH687.M294 2010
  799.17'57—dc22
                            2010014911

Contents

Acknowledgments

My mom always told me that you could tell a lot about people by looking at their shoes. While I don't pay much attention to shoes, I do believe that you can tell a lot about anglers by looking at their knots. I have been fortunate to have some of the finest fishing friends that a guy could hope for, and for the most part, their knots reflect that.

First, I would like to thank my great friend and fly-fishing mentor Dave Johnson for the countless hours of discussion on the fine points of knot tying and rigging. True expertise is like pure gold when doing a project like this. My thanks and admiration go out to Jay Nichols, Dusty Sprague, Jon Cave, and Howard Beemer for sharing theirs. In addition, I would like to thank Norm Zeigler, Chris Coile, Carl Kiesling, Eric Leiser, Joe Smith, and Mario Noche for their friendship, support, and strong opinions.

Most importantly, I would like to thank my wife, Yvonne, who wholeheartedly jumps into whatever crazy project I take on. And she doesn't even fish.

Knot-Tying Tips

Simplify. Learn to tie a few knots well. One of the goals of this book is to not only provide you with the best connections, but to also help you simplify your system.

* All knots should be lubricated with water before you pull them tight. Most anglers use saliva, though this has been shown to be unhealthy and may cause you to contract the *Giardia* parasite from contaminated water. Lip balm works very well for lubricating knots tied with larger diameter tippets, such as when tying blood knots in leader butt sections.

* When seating knots, pull them tight firmly and smoothly. Do not jerk them tight.

* After you seat the knot, test it with a slow, steady pull. It's better to know right then and there if an improperly tied knot is going to fail.

* When closing the knot, make sure that none of the turns overlap one another. These will weaken the knot.

* Knots are one weak point in a leader system, nicks and abrasions another. Periodically check your leader for abrasions or nicks by running your hands along it, especially after catching a fish or freeing a snag.

Practice your knots before you get on the water. Use two pieces of large rope (climbing rope is best because it is slick) or two pieces of old fly line to learn the knot and then repeat with larger (1X to 3X) tippet.

Trim all knots tightly, but take care not to nick them with your nippers. If you leave the tag ends long, they pick up moss, are more prone to tangling, and present a bulkier profile to the fish.

Until you master a knot, use plenty of tippet. Don't hobble your efforts trying to save a few cents.

Discard trimmings and used rigs properly. Several manufacturers sell miniature "garbage cans" that attach to your vest or lanyard, or you can make something similar. Either way, pack out your trimmings and trash.

Terminology

All tying steps in this book are for right-handers.

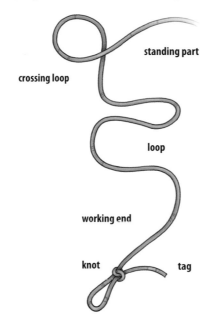

Standing part. The section of line that is not used to tie the knot itself. Generally speaking, not much of the standing part will be shown.

Crossing loop. A circle of line that passes over itself. (In some knot books, this is referred to as a "loop.")

Loop. A section of line that forms a U shape and does not cross itself. (In some knot books, this is called the "bight.")

Working end. The end of the line opposite the standing part.

Knot. The final configuration of line.

Tag. The end of line used to tie the knot, and the end of the line remaining beyond the knot that is usually trimmed away.

Lubricate. Moistening the knot before tightening (see note on page 1).

Dress. To remove slack by drawing the knot closed. This is where you will check that all is well before tightening. For example, on a clinch knot or blood knot, you want to make sure that there are no gaps between the wraps and the main line by pulling on the tag ends after tying the knot.

Tighten. The second-to-last stage of tying a knot, just before trimming any tag ends, where you firmly grasp and pull on the proper sections to draw the knot closed.

A QUESTION OF SCALE

As you read this book you may notice that I have taken liberty with scale in the illustrations. For example, you may say, "That fly looks *huge* in those hands," or perhaps the line seems too thick as it goes through the hook eye. I have done this in order to, as clearly as possible, make the steps easy to follow. In the leader formula and dropper illustrations, I have maintained "relative scale," meaning that if one section of line looks longer than another, then that's how it should be.

1

Attaching Backing and Fly Line

Backing serves two functions on a fly reel. First, it increases the diameter of the arbor. This ensures your fly line is wrapped around the spool in larger circles, which reduces memory in the line. If you were to just wrap the fly line around a bare arbor, you would have lots of small curls in it. This is called "memory." Also, when you increase the diameter of the arbor, each revolution of the reel takes in more line than it would on a bare arbor. This makes retrieving line more efficient.

The second thing that backing does is pack on 75 or more yards of insurance against a fish that runs far. This rarely happens on most streams, but on some rivers, like the Henry's Fork or the Missouri, you might just see your backing. In these situations, the knots you use to connect the backing to the reel spool and the backing to the fly line are critical.

Two types of backing are commonly available: gel spun polyethylene (GSP) and Dacron. Dacron is less expensive, easier to handle and tie knots with, and all you will need for trout. Be sure not to overload your reel with backing.

Uni Knot

For years the arbor knot was the recommended way to attach backing to the reel spool, and it still does a great job. But this is the arbor knot's only use. To attach the backing, let's use the versatile uni knot, also called the Duncan loop, because you can also use this knot to attach your leader to fly line (page 23), connect two tippets (page 42), and attach your fly to the tippet (page 59).

1 Pass 6 to 8 inches of tag end around the spool arbor and form a crossing loop.

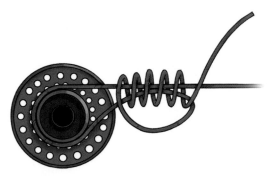

2 Wrap the tag around the standing line and top leg of the loop four to six times.

3 Pull the tag to tighten the wraps around the standing line.

4 Pull the standing line until the knot is snug against the arbor.

5 Pull on the tag to seat the knot. Trim the tag.

Double Surgeon's Loop

Once you have wound the backing tightly on the spool, you could tie it directly to the fly line with a nail knot (see page 11), but a loop-to-loop connection provides the flexibility of switching fly lines quickly and easily. The double surgeon's loop is a great choice for forming a loop in the backing because you can tie it easily and it will go through the rod guides smoothly. A 10-inch loop should be large enough to fit comfortably over your entire reel. You can also use this knot to connect the tippet to the leader with a loop-to-loop connection.

1 Double the line to form a loop that is large enough to slip over your reel, plus a few extra inches, and hold the two lines together.

2 Form a simple overhand knot, keeping the two lines together.

3 Pass the loop through the overhand knot three more times (totaling four wraps).

4 Tighten by pulling on the loop and the standing line. Pull on the tag and trim. Some people slip the loop around a nail hammered into their workbench and use pliers to pull on the tag.

Nail-Knot Loop

If you are like me, you'll enjoy the flexibility of changing lines and leaders without retying. The loop-to-loop system is just the ticket. Because of their rounded nature, fly line loops will travel through the guides smoothly in either direction. Most loops are also relatively watertight, preventing the ends of floating fly lines from absorbing water and sinking. Many lines now come with factory-made loops (on the back and front), but it is still good to know how to create them yourself.

Perhaps the most easily tied loop is the nail-knot loop. You make the nail-knot loop by forming a bend in the fly line and making a nail knot around it using a length of monofilament. If desired, a second nail knot can be tied on the bend. When finished, the loop should be approximately ¾ to 1 inch long. The small red stirring straws cut to 1 inch or so are perfect tools for forming the nail knot.

In a trout rig, the best use of the nail-knot loop is for creating a loop in your running line, to which you can attach your backing with a loop-to-loop connection. For heavier line weights and presentations where delicacy is not paramount, you can use the nail-knot loop to create a loop in the front of your line for attaching your leader, though there are more streamlined alternatives.

Supplies: 12 inches of 15-pound monofilament, small metal or plastic tube, flexible glue

1 Trim the end of the fly line at a 45-degree angle. This makes for a smoother connection that travels freely through the guides. Form a loop in the fly line.

2 Place the fly line loop just beyond the tube. Position the monofilament on top of the fly line and wrap around the fly line and tube one time.

3 Continue wrapping toward the loop (back over the monofilament) until you have a total of six wraps. Place the coils close to each other to make the knot easier to tighten.

4 While holding the wraps tightly, insert the tag end of the monofilament into the tube and push it through. Gently remove the tube.

5 Dress and lubricate the coils. Tighten them firmly by pulling on both ends of the monofilament.

6 Trim both ends of the monofilament. Add a drop of Zap-A-Gap, clear fingernail polish, or flexible cement such as Pliobond to the knot if you wish.

Braided Loop

Braided loops built from braided monofilament slip over
the end of the fly line, where they act like Chinese finger puzzles, tightening as they are pulled. Attach a loop
large enough to slip over a reel or fly line coil to the running line end of your fly line to make changing fly lines a
snap. On the front of the fly line, use this loop for your
sinking lines and shooting heads but not for floating lines—
the braided mono holds more water than other materials.

The best braided monofilament material to use for
lighter trout fly lines is either the Gudebrod 20- to 35-pound
Braided Butt Leader or Cortland 20- to 30-pound Braided
Mono. You can use a bobbin threader or make your own
splicing needle with a thin, stiff piece of wire such as a gui-
tar string (high E). Lefty Kreh, in *Fishing Knots*, recommends a size 2 to 4 section of trolling wire connected to a
large split ring with a haywire twist. Make sure to pinch the
ends of the wire into a point that threads easily through the
braided monofilament.

*Supplies: bobbin threader or homemade splicing needle,
20- to 30-pound braided monofilament, 12 inches of 10- to
12-pound monofilament or bobbin and thread, Pliobond*

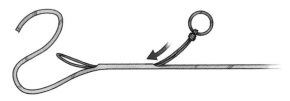

1 Pull off a length of braided monofilament (15 inches for a small loop, 30 inches for a large loop). Insert the bobbin threader (or splicing needle) into the braided monofilament and run it through the line 1½ to 2 inches and then out the other side of the line. Where you insert the needle determines how much of the finger trap you'll have to thread on your line when the loop is finished. It is better to have too much than too little, as you can always trim it to size before you slip it over the fly line.

2 Insert the end of the braided monofilament into the threader opening. Trim the braid with scissors so that no more than ⅛ inch sticks out.

3 Gently pull the end completely through and back out of the braid's core, massaging the braided core while you do this to help it through. Continue to pull the long end through the core until the loop is properly sized. Lefty Kreh suggests putting a small dowel (or pencil) in the loop to prevent pulling it through.

4 Once you have the loop size you desire, trim the tag end sticking out from the side of the braided monofilament core so that it is no more than 1½ inches long. Reinsert the needle through the braided line.

5 Run the tag through the braided line again to form a double catch, less than ¼ inch.

6 Grasp the loop and stretch the entire length of braided monofilament to smooth it out. Cut the tag flush with the braided monofilament sleeve.

7 Insert the end of the fly line into the braided monofilament and inchworm it in until it meets the ends of the buried tag ends of the loop.

8 Tie a nail knot or whip-finish with a bobbin and thread (see page 30, whipped loop) just beyond where the fly line enters the braid with the 10- to 12-pound-test monofilament. Trim the tag ends of the braid close to the knot. Coat the nail knot with Pliobond.

Connecting Loops

Whether connecting backing to fly line, fly line to leader, or sometimes even tippet to leader, you will use the versatile loop-to-loop connection frequently. Pay special attention when closing the connection so that it forms a square knot and not a girth hitch, which can weaken the connection.

1 Insert the loop of backing (created here with a double surgeon's loop, page 9) through the loop of fly line (created here with a nail knot, page 11).

2 Place the backing loop over the reel or spool.

3 Continue over the reel and pull the backing loop through the fly line loop.

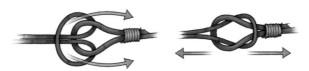

4 Draw the connection tight. You may end up with a girth hitch, which will weaken the line. If so, simply dress the knot by flipping the loop of backing over to form a square knot. Pull snug.

2

Fly Line to Leader

In trout fishing, the connection between your fly line and leader should not only be strong, it should also be straight for the best accuracy. Also, you do not want it to be bulky. Not only will cumbersome connections splash more than slim ones, but they may not slide easily through the guides and can possibly break delicate tippets. With larger fly lines, many anglers favor loops. We present here both options so that you can experiment and see what works best for you. While these knots are best tied at a well-lit workbench, far removed from the excitement of rising fish that can cause trembling fingers, it is important to be able to tie this connection in the field. So even if you like the streamlined Zap-A-Gap splice (page 25), know how to tie a nail knot in case of emergency.

Nail Knot

The nail knot is the time-honored method for attaching fly line to leader. While it does require retying when changing leaders, this connection is a good choice for gentle presentations and is very helpful when picking up grass and other floating debris is a concern. Some nail-knot tools on the market are worth trying if this is your preferred method of attaching leader butt to fly line, if only because they easily attach to your lanyard or vest so that you can find them easily.

Supplies: small metal or plastic tube (or nail-knot tool), flexible cement such as Pliobond

1 Place the fly line just beyond the tube. Position the butt end of the leader on top of the fly line, and wrap it around the fly line and tube one time.

2 Continue wrapping toward the end of the fly line (back over the leader itself) until you have a total of six wraps. Placing the coils close together makes it easier to close the knot. Use your fingers to pinch the coils in place.

3 While holding the wraps tightly, insert the tag end of the leader into the tube and push it through.

4 Gently remove the tube while continuing to pinch the coils. Dress and lubricate the coils. Tighten firmly by pulling on both ends of the leader.

5 Trim the tag end of the leader and excess fly line. Add a flexible cement such as Pliobond to the knot to smooth out the connection.

Nail-Less Nail Knot

Gary Borger's twist on this variation of the uni knot makes the finished knot look as good as a true nail knot. It is a real workhorse in the field when you can't find your small tube or nail-knot tool.

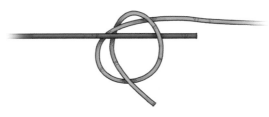

1 Form an overhand loop in the leader butt, adjacent to the end of the fly line. You will be sliding the knot down the line before tightening it, so don't worry too much about precise placement right now.

2 Take four to five wraps depending on the thickness of the leader material (the thicker it is, the fewer wraps you need.) This is the same as when tying a uni knot.

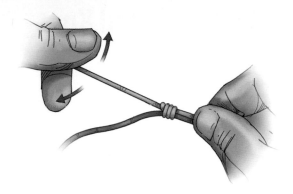

3 Here's the twist. Holding the long end of the leader material and the end of the fly line, pull the short end of the leader butt and twist it away from you as you pull. As the knot tightens it will be 6 inches or so above the end of the line. No problem. Slide the loose knot to where you want it. Borger pinches the end of the fly line and then slides the coils of the knot down with the fingers on his other hand, continuing to pull on both ends to take out the slack.

4 Pull hard on both ends to make sure the knot is tight. Clip off the tag end and the excess fly line.

Zap-A-Gap Splice

This elegant connection popularized by Dave Whitlock requires no knots and is perfect for light line weights where delicacy is paramount, and it glides easily through the guides when landing a fish. This connection is best made at home because of the tools required.

Supplies: Zap-A-Gap, #9 crewel needle, pin vise or small pliers, 100-grit sandpaper or emery board, razor blade, 3X to 6X knotless leader

1 Place the tip of the needle in a pin vise (or pliers) and push the needle eye through the center of the fly-line core, approximately $^3/_8$ inch, and then out the side of the fly line.

2 Thread the tippet portion of the leader through the eye. If you have difficulty threading the tippet, trim it at an angle using a razor blade.

3 Pull the leader through the fly line until about 2 inches remain on the other side of the fly line.

4 Roughen up ³⁄₈ inch of the leader in front of the fly line until it is opaque. Tie an overhand knot at the butt end of the leader for gripping.

5 Place a drop of Zap-A-Gap on the roughened-up section and pull on the leader butt sharply, pulling the roughened-up section into the fly line.

6 Trim the leader butt flush, place a drop of Zap-A-Gap on the hole, and pull on the leader so that the butt goes inside the fly line.

Zap-A-Gap Loop

Developed by fly-fishing great Dave Whitlock, this sleek loop, formed with the core of the fly line, tucks back into the fly line, leaving no visible knots or wraps. Exposing the core allows water to seep in, so this one is best used on sinking lines and shooting heads. The finished loop length should be approximately ³/₄ to 1 inch.

Supplies: nail-polish remover containing acetone, small scissors, #8 or #9 needle (dulled), needle threader (optional), pin vise or pliers, 12 inches of 10- to 12-pound monofilament, Pliobond

1 Soak 5 to 6 inches of the fly-line tip in nail-polish remover for 30 minutes. Strip off the coating with your fingernails, exposing the core.

2 Fray the ends of the braided core with a needle and brush out the individual strands. Cut out half of the fibers so that you can thread the remaining ones through the needle.

3 Insert the dulled needle into the core where the exposed core meets the fly-line coating. Push the needle into the fly line $3/8$ inches and $1/2$ inch out the other side of the fly line.

4 Wet the core filaments, and pass them through the eye of the needle (or use a needle threader). Use a pin vise or pliers to pull the needle and core through the fly line and out.

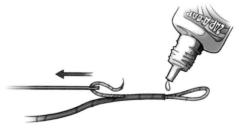

5 Continue to pull on the core until the braided loop is a little larger than you want it. Apply a bit of Zap-A-Gap at the base of the loop.

6 Pull on the core end a little more to pull the Zap-A-Gap inside the fly line, welding the loop core inside the fly line. Cut the excess braided core flush with the exit hole. Pull hard on the loop and fly line to stretch and pull the tip inside the fly line.

Whipped Loop

A well-whipped loop is stronger than the fly line itself and is virtually watertight. Be sure to spend a little extra time preparing for and building this one, as it will last a long time and you will want it to be just right. Ideal uses are for forming loops in the backing ends of all trout lines (make the loop large) or as a loop on the front of larger trout lines (5-weight and heavier), especially nymph and streamer lines where precise and delicate presentations are not paramount (for dry-fly lines, use the nail knot).

Supplies: razor blade, bobbin loaded with heavier fly-tying thread (3/0, 6/0, 140- or 210-denier), 10-inch length of 6- to 8-pound-test monofilament (optional), Pliobond

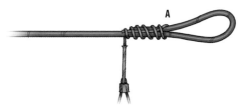

1 Pull approximately 12 inches of thread through the bobbin. Remove the thread spool and make five turns of thread around one leg of the bobbin (this will keep tension on the bobbin spool while you swing it to ensure tight wraps). Slice the end of the fly line at a 45-degree angle, or thinner, with the razor blade for a smooth transition.

Form a tight loop in the fly line, leaving at least 1 inch of doubled line to wrap over. With your left hand, pinch the end of the thread from the bobbin and both of the doubled over ends of the fly line at the area marked "A." With your right hand, grasp the bobbin and wrap over the thread end until the thread and bobbin dangle from the fly line unaided. This jam knot is the same one that you would use to attach the thread to the hook shank if you were tying a fly.

2 Once the thread is securely attached, spin the bobbin by moving both of your hands in a forward motion, wrapping the thread between your two hands. Guiding the thread with your hands, slowly work down the transition area.

3 Once the loop is secure, start swinging the bobbin around the doubled line, making enough wraps (approximately 50) to cover the 1 inch of doubled line and the tapered end. The faster you swing the bobbin, the tighter the wraps will be.

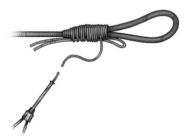

4 To tie an easy whip-finish knot, place a loop of monofilament along the thread wraps. Make a dozen more wraps over the monofilament.

5 Break the thread and pass it through the monofila-ment loop.

6 Pull the thread under the wraps, forming the whip-finish knot. Coat the wraps with Pliobond.

Perfection Loop

Quick and easy to tie, this loop will align as a perfectly straight extension of the leader, which is why many prefer it over the (arguably) easier-to-tie double surgeon's loop, which is bulkier and not in-line. Because it is slim and straight, it is ideal for use at the butt of the leader, or as the loop when connecting leader to tippet to extend the life of your store-bought leader (see page 64).

1 Form a crossing loop.

2 Form a second crossing loop behind the first loop. The size of the second loop will determine the size of the finished knot. Pull the tag end straight down between the two loops.

3 Reach in and pull the back loop through the front loop.

4 Tighten by pulling the end of the loop and the standing line in opposite directions. Put your finger inside the loop to pull it tight, and use the rounded edges of forceps or pliers to seat it firmly. Trim the tag.

3

Connecting Tippets and Building Leaders

On a trout stream you often have to deal with fine tippets that can be hard to handle, so it is important to choose and master a knot that you can tie confidently—even in adverse conditions such as low light and cold weather. As you decrease the size of the tippets, knot strength becomes paramount. Remember your entire system is only as strong as the weakest links, which are the knot that you use to attach your fly and the knot that you use to attach your tippets.

Surgeon's Knot

A perfect balance of strength and simplicity, this is my go-to knot when I need to change tippet or build a leader quickly and easily (such as in low-light conditions). I also prefer this knot when attaching a fluorocarbon tippet. The surgeon's knot, by definition, is only two turns, while a double surgeon's is four turns. For 6-pound-test monofilament or less, I recommend the double surgeon's. This knot is better than the standard blood knot at joining lines of widely differing diameters.

1 Place the two lines together with working ends opposite each other.

2 Tie a simple overhand knot keeping the two lines together.

3 Pass the two lines through again for a surgeon's (shown). Simply pass the two lines through one more time for increased security in lighter tippets. Lubricate.

4 Tighten by pulling on all four strands (two tags and two standing lines). The finished knot should resemble a figure eight.

Surgeon's Shortcut

Here is a way to tie the surgeon's knot with your eyes closed.

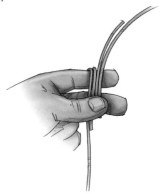

1 Wrap the two strands around slightly spread fingers.

2 Make a second wrap and pass the lines through the loops. Lubricate and tighten by pulling all four strands.

Blood Knot

The blood knot, also known as the barrel knot, is a sleek, symmetrical knot used for joining lines of similar diameters. This one, for good reason, is the most popular knot for building leaders. If you are joining lines with dissimilar diameters, the surgeon's knot is a better choice, or you can tie an improved blood knot by doubling over the thinner-diameter line and tying the regular blood knot with it.

1 Place the two lines together with the working ends opposite each other.

2 Take the working end of line A five times around line B. Pass the active working end between the two lines. Pinch with the thumb and forefinger to maintain this gap.

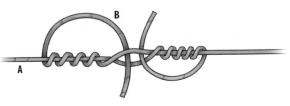

3 Wrap the working end of line B around line A five times. Insert the tag of line B in the gap opposite the tag of line A. It is crucial that the two lines enter the gap in opposite directions or the knot will fail.

4 Place the two tag ends between your teeth, lubricating the wraps at the same time, and slowly pull the standing lines in opposite directions.

5 Trim the tag ends and test the knot.

Uni to Uni

Y ou can also use the versatile uni to build or add tippet to your leader. When finished, the uni to uni knot resembles a blood knot and is equally strong—the difference is that the tags come out of each end of the knot, rather than the middle.

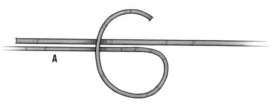

1 Place the two lines together with working ends opposite each other. Bend tag A around to form a loop.

2 Pass the tag through the loop four to six times.

3 Pull tag A and standing line A enough to make the knot snug but do not tighten too much.

4 Repeat the procedure using line B in the opposite direction. Lubricate both knots. Pull on the two standing lines to slide the two knots together.

5 Tighten by pulling on all four strands. Trim the tags.

Seaguar Knot

This knot, which I first saw in Lefty Kreh's *Fishing Knots*, is an effective way to make a connection that is stronger than a surgeon's knot and easier to tie. In heavier tippets, you can just use your pointer finger instead of forceps. The line manufacturer Seaguar recommends this knot for fluorocarbon.

1 Place the leader and tippet together with working ends opposite each other and form a loop. Hold the leader and tippet firmly together.

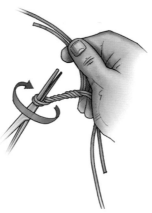

2 Insert the forceps into the loop and make three twists.

3 Gently grasp the leader and tippet.

4 Pull down through the loop.

5 Remove the forceps and dress and lubricate the knot. Tighten by pulling first on all four strands and finally by pulling on the two standing lines. Trim the tags.

Tippet-to-Fly Knots

This is the end of the line, literally. Because the tippets used in trout fishing are so fine, this is the weakest link in your entire system. Here are a few important points to consider. The best knot is one that you can tie consistently well. In informal tests with a line tester, even the simple clinch frequently failed at widely dissimilar breaking strengths, pointing to either inconsistencies in tippet material (perhaps) or inconsistencies in technique (more likely).

Also, most of these knots are strong enough for most trout. Ultra-thin tippets (6X to 8X) aside, if the knot is tied well and there are no abrasions or nicks in the line to weaken it, then chances are you will not apply enough pressure on the fish to break the knot. Some 5X fluorocarbon tests at 5 pounds breaking strength, which is more pressure than most can apply with a bent fly rod. Try it at home. What most often breaks your tippet is a jerk, not a slow, steady pull.

You can conduct informal tests by attaching a fly to either end of a length of tippet (12 inches or so) with two different knots, and then pulling on both of them at the same time to see which breaks first. When doing this, grasp the hook bends with pliers and wear glasses.

Improved Clinch Knot

The improved clinch, to me, is the '57 Chevy of knots. There are sleeker and stronger knots, but this one is the classic. When properly tied, seated, and *tightened*, the improved clinch works well with smaller-diameter lines. It does not test as strong as some other tippet-to-fly knots, but many guides favor it because they can tie it quickly and more consistently than other, more complicated knots. In fact, many argue that the even easier clinch, which only requires passing the tag through the loop closest to the eye of the fly and not the large loop, is stronger, especially with fluorocarbon tippets. Try both and see what works best for you.

1 Thread the line through the eye of the hook and begin to wrap it around the standing line.

2 Make a total of five turns around the standing line and pass the tag through the loop that was formed near the eye.

3 Pass the tag through the second, larger loop that is now formed. Lubricate and pull gently on the tag to pull the knot together. Make sure that the coils do not overlap.

4 Tighten by pulling on both the standing line and the tag. Trim the tag.

Fisherman's Knot

This knot is also called the Pitzen and 16-20, among other names. Whatever you choose to call it, this "reversed clinch" is easily tied and stronger and smaller than the improved clinch. However, it does require you to use more tippet and some find it harder to tie than the improved clinch—though I provide some tips for making it easier. With one simple variation—passing the tag end through the loop formed at the hook eye like you would for an improved clinch knot (see step 2, page 49)—you get another version of the knot, often called the Heiliger or San Diego jam.

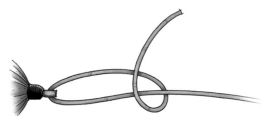

1 Insert the tippet through the eye of the hook and form a crossed loop around the standing line.

2 Make three to five wraps around the both lines, wrapping back toward the hook.

3 After making the wraps, take the tag and pass through the back of the loop opposite the hook.

4 Lubricate and dress so that the wraps lie neatly together. Tighten by pulling firmly on the standing line. When the knot is tied properly, you will see it pop into place. Trim the tag.

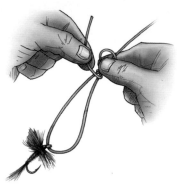

TIP: One way to make this knot easier to tie is by threading 4 to 6 inches of tippet through the eye of the fly, pinching the loop with your right hand, and then making the wraps back toward the fly with your left hand. If you want to impress your friends, you can clamp forceps on to the hook bend and swing the fly around as you wrap—similar to how bass pros tie this knot with spinner baits.

Art Scheck, in *Fly Fish Better*, recommends hooking the fly on a zipper pull or large snap swivel attached to a zipper. This frees both hands to tie this knot. You can use this trick for other knots too!

Orvis (Becker) Knot

The Orvis Company once set out to find the strongest knot for attaching the fly to the tippet. Larry Becker of Rockford, Illinois, answered the call. Here is Becker's creation, a small, strong variation of a figure-eight knot that is easily tied and uses little tippet material.

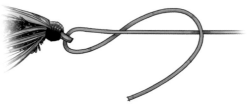

1 Pass the line through the eye of the hook. Pass the line behind the standing line and to the front again.

2 Pass the tag through the back side of the first loop, and then through the back side of the second loop.

3 Make two wraps around the second loop. Lubricate.

4 Draw the knot nearly closed by pulling the fly and tag apart. Release the tag and finish tightening by pulling fly and standing line firmly. Trim the tag.

Forceps Clinch

The forceps clinch is a great way to add a dropper to a dry fly. Using forceps also makes this knot easier to tie in cold weather. You may also twist the tippet with your index finger—stick your thumb through the hole, grab the tag, and pull it through.

1 Form an open loop in the tippet and insert the forceps with the jaws closed.

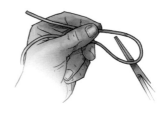

2 Twist the loop five times with the forceps.

3 Open up the jaws of the forceps and grasp the tag end.

4 Pull the tag down through the loop. Draw the knot slightly, making sure to leave the loop open.

5 Remove the forceps, lubricate, and place the hook point through the loop.

6 Tighten by pulling the fly and standing line in opposite directions.

Non-Slip Loop

A loop connection to streamers and nymphs allows a free-swinging action that eliminates the stiff, mechanical connection that I call a "Puppet Show." When the non-slip loop is finished the tag points toward the hook and is less likely to pick up grass or other flotsam. In my opinion, the smaller the loop, the better. The size of the gap between the loop and the hook determines the size of the finished loop. The number of wraps changes with the diameter. Here is what Lefty recommends in Fishing Knots: "For lines testing 8X to 6-pound-test, make seven turns; for 8- to 12-pound-test, make five turns; for 15- to 40-pound-test, four turns." For lines heavier than that (or wire), you only have to use three turns.

1 Tie a simple overhand knot in the line before passing the tag end through the eye of the hook.

2 Pass the tag through the overhand knot the same way it came out. Pull gently on the tag until the overhand knot is near (¼ inch or less) the eye of the hook.

3 Make five turns (more for the lightest lines; less for heavier) around the standing line, working toward the hook. Pass the tag through the original overhand knot. Lubricate.

4 Tighten by pulling on the standing line, the tag, and the fly simultaneously. Trim the tag.

Duncan Loop

The Duncan loop is an adjustable loop knot formed from the uni knot. It is useful when you want to allow your subsurface flies to have more action, and it is handy for rigging the moveable dropper on page 73, which allows you to quickly and easily attach another fly to your nymphing system. Since it is a sliding loop (you can more or less close it tight and adjust the loop later), this knot is a good candidate if you like to rig your dropper nymphs ahead of time. Simply attach your nymph to 12 to 16 inches of tippet, tie a Duncan loop in the other end, and wrap them around a store-bought or homemade dropper holder.

1 Thread the tippet through the eye of the hook and bend the tag around to form a loop.

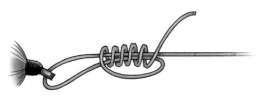

2 Pass the tag through the loop four to six times.

3 Pull the tag and the standing line but do not tighten the knot too much. Make sure the wraps are neatly lying next to each other. Lubricate the knot.

4 Pull on the standing line until the loop is the desired size, and then grasp the tag with forceps and pull firmly.

5 If you don't want a loop, continue to pull the standing line until the knot touches the eye of the hook. Grasp the tag, tighten, and trim the tag. When this knot is pulled tight, you have a uni knot, an adequate substitute for the clinch.

Eugene Bend

This knot uses more line than the clinch, but it is stronger. Though about as strong as the fisherman's (aka Pitzen or 16-20) knot, it is easier for some to tie and, unlike the fisherman's, it can be tied with forceps. Simply insert the jaws through the doubled-over loop, rotate them three times, and grasp the tag end with the forceps, pulling it through. Like the fisherman's, this knot pops into place when it is seated properly.

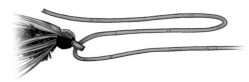

1 Pass the tippet through the eye of the hook and form a 6-inch open loop. You can pass the tippet through the top or the bottom of the eye, depending on your preference.

2 Wrap the loop around the standing line three times.

3 Pass the tag end through the loop.

4 Pull the tag end away from the hook to dress the knot. Lubricate it.

5 Pull the standing end of the line until the knot slides down the line to the fly. The knot will pop when it seats properly. Clip the tag.

5

Leaders

Covering the myriad leaders and leader formulas is beyond the scope of this little guide, but here are a few tips to help simplify the process. For basic dry-fly fishing, just use a store-bought leader and attach tippet as necessary. Since many strike indicators cause kinks in the butts of leaders, it is a good idea to have separate leaders for nymphing. A loop-to-loop system makes it easy to change between your dry-fly leader and your nymph leader. A properly cared for dry-fly leader can last an entire season.

Customizing
a Store-Bought Leader

Knotless trout leaders are convenient and perform well. To extend the life of a new leader (as much as an entire season), cut 24 inches from the tippet end and tie a loop knot such as a perfection (see page 34) or double surgeon's (page 9) in that end. Tie a loop knot in the end of the tippet you cut away and reattach it with a loop-to-loop connection. Replenish only the tippet section whenever it gets too short.

Incidentally, when removing a store-bought leader from its package, unwrap three or four turns of the thick end around the coils first. After you have unwrapped the butt, put your hand in the coils and stretch your fingers to keep tension on the coils. Continue to unwrap the thick end until the entire leader is uncoiled. Do not rush this process and don't try to just shake out the coils or chances are you will get a tangled mess. After it is uncoiled, straighten the entire leader by running it through your fingers several times.

loop-to-loop connection

George Harvey Leader

George Harvey's dry-fly leader is the foundation for most of today's leaders. Over the years, Harvey modified his leader design, changing from a stiff to supple butt. Lefty Kreh and others point out that the best leader butts for casting should have a flexible weight. The Harvey leader has two parts: the basic leader (which always stays the same) and the tippet section. The diagram here shows a formula for a 11-foot, 6-inch, 5X leader. A shorter leader tapering to 4X can be made by using 15 inches of 3X and 36 inches of 4X for the tippet.

The design of this leader and the length of the tippet in this formula ensure that the leader does not straighten out, leaving nice S curves in the line to reduce micro drag. Make this leader work best for you by accelerating to an abrupt stop on your forward cast and then dropping your arm and rod tip. Experiment until you see well-defined curves in the tippet in front of the fly.

George Harvey Leader

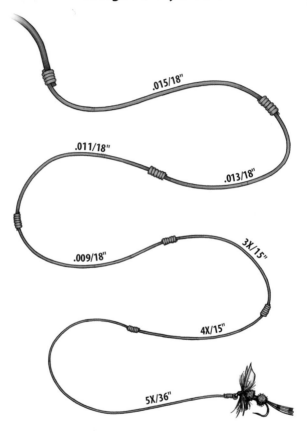

.015/18"

.011/18"

.013/18"

.009/18"

3X/15"

4X/15"

5X/36"

Harrop Dry-Fly Leader

René Harrop developed this 14-foot leader for the challenging conditions of the Henry's Fork, and it excels when casting small flies, especially when also contending with wind.

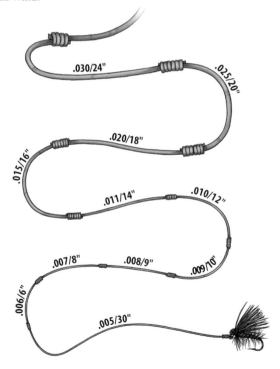

.030/24"

.025/20"

.020/18"

.015/16"

.011/14"

.010/12"

.007/8"

.008/9"

.009/10"

.006/6"

.005/30"

Hinged Leader

The hinged, or right-angle, leader allows the fly to drift directly below the strike indicator, at a 90-degree angle, which allows you to accurately follow the drift of the fly and easily detect strikes. You can use this system with a number of indicators, including yarn (shown) or Thingamabobbers. The heavy leader to the indicator turns a weighted rig and air-resistant indicator over easily, and the thin-diameter tippet to the fly allows it to sink quickly to the bottom.

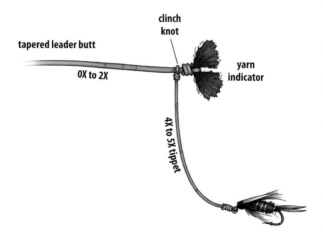

clinch knot

tapered leader butt

0X to 2X

yarn indicator

4X to 5X tippet

6

Rigs

Fishing two or more flies at a time is effective for several reasons. When you suspend one or more nymphs from a dry fly, you not only have a strike indicator that has the potential to hook fish, but you can cover several different areas in the water column. In low, clear water, fish often spook from the splash of a conventional strike indicator, making the dry and dropper a wise choice for situations where stealth is required. A buoyant strike indicator also allows you to fish several weighted nymphs in heavier currents, which increases your odds of hooking up by showing the fish different flies at different depths.

To prevent tangles, forget the conventional, snappy dry-fly cast with multiple-fly rigs—open your loops and slow down your casting stroke. Also, some anglers find that using the Belgian (aka oval) cast helps prevent tangles. Before fishing more than one fly, be sure that local regulations permit it.

Hook-Bend Dropper

clinch knot

4X–6X

12–36"

To add a nymph dropper to a dry fly, simply take the tippet connected to the dropper and tie it to the bend of the dry-fly hook with your favorite knot (such as the forceps clinch, page 55). The distance between the dry fly and nymph can range from 4 inches to 3 feet.

This rig shines in shallow water or when larger indicators spook wary fish. Not only is it effective with one or more nymphs (John Barr's hopper-copper-dropper system uses two nymphs below a buoyant hopper), but it is also effective with two dry flies. Use a larger fly to help you see a smaller one.

Midge Dropper

With this dropper method, you can change the top fly easily, and the loop knot allows you to use heavier tippet with smaller flies and still retain a natural presentation.

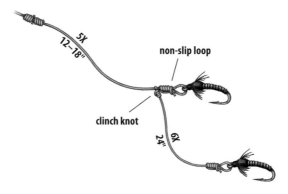

Connect a 12- to 18-inch piece of tippet to your leader. Attach the upper fly with a non-slip loop. Add 24 inches of smaller-diameter material using an improved clinch knot above the non-slip loop, tighten the clinch knot, and slide it down until the two knots touch. Tie the bottom fly on with a non-slip loop. In *Modern Midges*, Jeff Ehlert recommends using fluorocarbon tippet with this rig. When you want to change your top fly, simply slide the clinch knot up the tippet, snip the top fly off, tie on a new one, and slide the clinch knot down again.

Moveable Dropper

This rig from *Fishing Tandem Flies* allows you to quickly add a dropper to your setup using the Duncan loop. Attach your dropper fly to 4 to 6 inches of tippet with the knot of your choice (mine is the Becker). It doesn't matter whether you tie on the fly before or after creating the Duncan loop, you just want to make sure that the overall length of the dropper does not exceed 4 to 6 inches.

1 Pinch a loop of tippet with your left hand and form the beginning of the Duncan loop with your right hand.

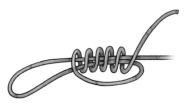

2 Continue to hold the loop while you wrap the tag end four to five times to form the Duncan loop. Make sure the loop is large enough to pass easily over the fly.

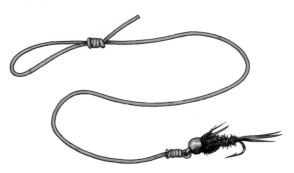

3 Put your finger in the loop and pull on the tag to close the wraps. (Do not pull it tight.)

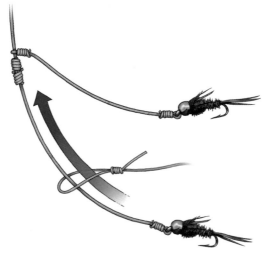

4 Pass the loop up over your fly and cinch it tight above a knot on your leader.

Eye-to-Eye Dropper

Many small-fly anglers like to connect their flies to the eyes of the hooks so that the gap is not obstructed by tippet, which many feel decreases the hooking capabilities. Another advantage that many cite is that the nymph rides in the water column differently than if it is connected to the bend of the first fly. Make sure that the lines come off of the sides of the hook's eye rather than the front.

Blood-Knot Dropper

This is a quick way to build a dropper into your leader. After tying a blood knot, clip only one of the tags, and then attach a nymph to the remaining one. When tying the knot, be sure to use enough tippet material to provide for a sufficiently long tag end (4 to 6 inches is standard).

7

Indicators

Strike indicators are an important part of the nymphing rig and must be matched to the water and lighting conditions, the weight of the flies you are using, and in some instances, fishing pressure. A dazzling array of store-bought indicators are available, though many anglers prefer the flexibility (and savings) of making their own.

Rubber Band and Yarn Indicator

Of all the strike-indicator materials, yarn is the most sensitive, and when treated generously with floatant, it is very buoyant. Using an orthodontic rubber band makes this indicator especially easy to adjust according to water depth. You can use yarn marketed for strike indicators, polypropylene craft cord available through craft supply stores, or macramé yarn such as Maxi-Cord or Bonnie Braid. Make a brush from a dowel and piece of Velcro for applying the floatant.

Supplies: forceps, scissors, small ($^5/_{16}$ inch) orthodontic rubber band, polypropylene craft cord or macramé yarn, small brush, fly floatant

1 Wrap the $^5/_{16}$-inch orthodontist rubber band 4 to 6 times around the tip of your hemostats. If you place the strike indicator near the butt end of the leader, you'll need fewer wraps to hold the strike indicator in place. It takes more wraps to keep the strike indicator in place as the leader decreases in diameter.

2 Form a U shaped loop by pinching the leader with your index finger and thumb. Open the tips of your forceps and grab the leader.

3 Slide the rubber band on to the leader, forming a loop.

4 Insert the yarn into the loop.

5 Slide the rubber band snug against the yarn.

6 Trim the yarn to the size you desire. Heavy nymphs or turbulent currents require more yarn.

7 Brush fly floatant in thoroughly with a fluffing tool.

8 Pull on both sides of the leader to seat. Refluff the yarn as needed and reapply floatant whenever the yarn begins to absorb water and sink.

Slip Knot and Yarn Indicator

This indicator excels when you want to rig a yarn indicator quickly or don't want to fuss with rubber bands. If you need to change the depth of your indicator frequently, such as when fishing pocketwater, then it is better to go with a system that doesn't kink your leader as much as this one. For instructions on making a quick slip knot, see page 84.

Supplies: yarn, scissors, small brush, floatant

1 Form a crossing loop in the leader.

2 Form a second crossing loop *behind* the first.

3 Pull the back loop through the front loop to form the slip knot. For a shortcut, see page 84, the two-finger slip knot.

4 Insert the yarn into the slip-knot loop.

5 Pull the leader on each side of the slip knot to seat the knot.

6 Trim the yarn to length.

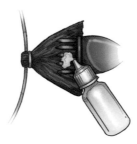

7 Brush floatant in thoroughly.

8 The indicator is now ready to go.

Two-Finger Slip Knot

Here is the quickest and easiest way to form a slip knot, useful for the indicator on page 81.

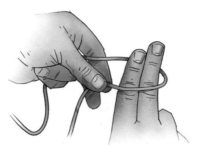

1 Form an open loop and insert your index and middle fingers (palm out).

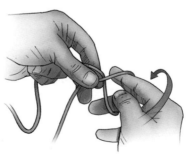

2 Twist your fingers downward.

3 Reach in and grasp the lower standing line.

4 Pull firmly outward to form the slip knot.

Thingamabobber Strike Indicator

Thingamabobbers ride high, are reusable and adjustable, and will float the heaviest rigs, even in turbulent water. They are available in a wide range of sizes and colors. Try them in different colors for different light conditions. Tip: White blends well into the foam on the water's surface.

1 Form an open loop and insert the loop into the hole in the Thingamabobber.

2 Pass the loop over the ball portion.

3 Pull the leader on each side of Thingamabobber to tighten. Make sure to seat the loop around the shoulders of the indicator to prevent it from slipping.

Thingamabobber Band Indicator

Using a small orthodontic rubber band prevents the Thingamabobber from kinking your leader while still allowing you to adjust it easily.

1 Pass the looped end of a small rubber band through the hole at the bottom of the indicator and back through the loop in the rubber band, forming a girth hitch.

2 To attach the indicator to the leader, pass the rubber band around the indicator.

3 Keep wrapping the band around the indicator, three or four times, until the band is tight on the leader butt.

4 This setup does not kink your leader.

Balloon Strike Indicator

The balloon indicator is an inexpensive strike indicator that is among the most buoyant, which is particularly useful in turbid waters or when fishing heavy nymphs. It is cheaper than a Thingamabobber, casts easier in the wind than a large yarn indicator, and is a sure conversation starter on the water. Keep the balloons small, about the size of a quarter.

1 Inflate a small, round party balloon to approximately the size of a quarter. Tie off.

2 Form a slip knot and place the loop around the balloon stem.

3 Pull the leader ends on each side of the slip knot.

4 Trim the balloon stem just below the knot.

Index